Praise for *You A...*

"In this wonderful book, Colin Boyd ...
sensitise to and gain useful understanding of the infinite vista of experience
that is touch. This is an exceedingly accessible book for all. I have no
hesitation as a qualified health practitioner in recommending to you to
explore this book, practice the exercises and feel the changes in your life."

— **Frederick W. Court** B.HSc, Dip.Arts
Registered Chinese Medicine Practitioner & Acupuncturist

"Colin's 'You Are Touch' offers some of the oldest forms of traditional
Qigong practices in a new light, one based on a more feeling awareness of
the essence of these practices so that rather than just being a sterile physical
exercise they become a process of allowing the body to deeply feel in touch
with what he calls 'The Radiant Field of All-Pervading Energy'."

— **Paul Litchfield** and **Jane Yang Wujichigong**, Australia

"Colin's understanding of touch comes from many years of dedicated practice
and a deep devotion to his teacher. His treatments are transformational and
yet so simple. Thank you Colin!"

— **Liz Arundel**, international Shiatsu teacher and Tai Chi student

"Colin's book, *You Are Touch*, brings real instruction on how to connect
with this 'waking essence' from the body through to the mind and into the
'Heart of being Itself'."

— **Jym Daly**, Artistic Director of Fidget Feet, award-wining international
theatre company

"I was fascinated by the part that discussed about listening to heartbeat and breathing. And if you are a seeker of sort, then you get to obtain a free lecture about reality and being as well... in simple words."

— **Marisse Lee**, Writer, *Harping by a Pixie* (blog)

"In responding to Colin's book, I can feel the essence of 'Intrinsic Touch Energy' practice is to know embodied awareness as expansion and depth non-verbally. With this comes boundlessness. Such is the mystery of this intriguing book 'You Are Touch'."

— **Lynne Thompson**, Somatic Body-Worker and Dance Teacher

"Colin's "Intrinsic Touch Energy" session embodied from his book *You Are Touch* gave me a sense of energetic connection through the words and movement that helped me to feel the natural life flow of energy itself."

— **Gavin Brown**, Psychiatric Nurse / Author

"Movement, awareness and energy flow and also integrating Adi's Da's words in there too. How fantastic!"

— **Dean Steadman**, Photographer

"These exercise routines are not routine! This is happiness, spontaneity, freedom, a discipline of play and fun! Let me suggest that Colin's 'Intrinsic Touch' is an invitation to touch and be touched by the cosmic unity, in prior harmony with the all pervading energy, the love that fills and is our every breath."

— **Simon Pritchard**, Artist

You
Are
Touch

rebalance body and mind
with the simple new practice of
Intrinsic Touch Energy

ITE

Colin Boyd

SILVER SNAKE PRESS

DISCLAIMER

Information in this book is not intended to replace the services of a trained healthcare professional or serve as a replacement for medical care. Consult your physician or healthcare professional before following the author's proposed courses of exercise. Any application of the methods described in this book is at the reader's discretion and sole risk.

Published by Silver Snake Press, Wellington

www.silversnakepress.com

Cover design by Julien Lesage

ISBN 978-0-473-57036-1 (paperback)

This book is dedicated

to

the Life,

Spiritual Teaching

and

Blessing Work

of

Adi Da Samraj

First and foremost, my gratitude goes to the Divine World Teacher, Adi Da Samraj (1939-2008), whom I am indebted to.

Adi Da's revelation of truth on the profound nature of touch as a healing modality is the principal reason why I wrote this book. The sensibility to know "touch" in the manner herein presented is only one of the many gifts Adi Da communicates and reveals to all who recognise and respond to his radiant sign of blessing, freely offered to the world.

Adi Da is the guiding light that awakened my heart to true love, freedom and happiness. I could not have known such freedom existed without first coming into contact with him through his revelatory word and spiritual wisdom, which is the basis of my life as a student of his "Reality-Way" of Adidam.

Adi Da is the very essence and core of this book. Any benefits gained by the reader are attributed to Adi Da as the ultimate and final source and substance of everything I have herein written.

Every insight, understanding and clarity that came through this writing is based on following Adi Da's revelation word and spiritual teachings.

Many periods of sitting in his spiritually-blessed company along with significant time spent in his spiritual sanctuaries and places of unique blessing power gave me the inspiration to complete this book.

In short, Adi Da is the soul and purpose that inspired my heart to write this book. It is an expression of what I feel is the deep significance of "touch" as a modality for initiating great and positive change in the world as well as potentially bringing a greater degree of peace, love and radiant calm into our daily lives.

www.adidasamraj.org

In the Most Perfect Stand of Consciousness Itself, there is no "me", no "someone" egoically "self"-identified with the body, no "subjective" awareness "somewhere inside" (being confronted by the "outside world" of apparently "objective" conditional manifestation).

In the Most Perfect Stand of Consciousness Itself, you Realize that you Stand in the Indivisible Domain of Infinite Energy--and you Realize that every conditionally apparent being, thing, and event is simply an apparent modification of Infinite Energy. In the Most Perfect Stand of Consciousness Itself, you do not even encounter the body-except as an apparent modification of Infinite Energy.

In the Position of Consciousness Itself, It Is Intrinsically Self-Evident That There Is Only Consciousness Itself In and As the Indivisible Domain of Infinite Energy. All kinds of beings, things, and events are arising conditionally, but they are only apparent modifications of the Self-Radiant Energy of Self-Existing Consciousness - or Divine and One and Indivisible and Perfectly egoless and Perfectly Acausal Conscious Light.

This Is "Perfect Knowledge".
This Is the "Knowledge" That Is Perfect Divine Enlightenment.

Adi Da Samraj – The Aletheon

Contents

You Are Touch

Every day of our lives
we have never felt a moment
when this is not true

Every moment in your life
is an opportunity
to rediscover
what touches you

Intrinsically

We will explore
into
through
and as
the

Touch "Sensory" Space

An excursion
without face
or self-image
A space where
the heart
can be
set free

Consciously

Introduction

No matter where we are or what we are doing, each of us is, in every moment, already participating in feeling as touch, just by virtue of being alive. While we might not know what touch is exactly, or how universal it is, touch is still an essential part of all of our lives, all of the time.

When we think of touch, most of us think of it as one of the five senses, the perceptual faculty we use to make physical contact with something. But touch, as you will discover reading this book, is so much more than that. Touch is accessed through our natural state of awareness. It is not just something we "do" in relation to others or things, nor is it limited by physical proximity. Touch is a living process that we inhabit. In other words touch is not only something we're doing, touch is what we <u>are</u>.

Touch is everywhere. Think of the technology we use every day to stay connected – mobile phones and the internet, for instance. People often say things like "let's stay in touch" without necessarily thinking of the root sensitivity or meaning of their words. The use of your voice over a mobile phone, for instance, is a subtler but no less tangible form of vibratory touch felt physically by the recipient.

One of the reasons I was inspired to write this book is based on a single statement by my spiritual teacher Adi Da Samraj. He said that "touch is the primary sensation". From Adi Da's perspective touch is the primary sensation of all the sensations because of its relationship to the body as a whole. In the book 'Conductivity Healing' compiled from his direct instructions on the process of healing he states:

Human beings have several bodily senses, most of which are localized through a specific organ. Seeing is, in general, localized through the eyes, hearing through the ears, smelling through the nose, and tasting through the mouth - but the entire body is an organ of touch. In terms of its comprehensiveness then, the body is the senior sense organ, and the sense of touch is the means whereby just about anyone can very quickly become aware of the aura of the etheric energy-field of the body.

Avatar Adi Da Samraj
"The Body As Energy and The Universal Field of Consciousness"
The Transmission of Doubt

Therefore touch is also primary due to its relationship to this energy field. He states further:

The process whereby you achieve sensitivity to this energy-field is through the primary sense of touch, or through feeling-contact. The other senses may play a part in this sensitivity to, or observation of the etheric-field, but the primary organ of "self"-awareness in terms of the energy-field or etheric body is your feeling-capability. And your feeling-capability is an extension of the sense of touch.

Avatar Adi Da Samraj
"Early-Life Education, or, My Seventh Stage Way of Schooling In The First Three Stages of Life"
The First Three Stages of Life

Central to this new understanding of touch is an understanding of the universal nature of energy. Energy, as yogis and mystics have long known, and as quantum physicists are now discovering, is universal and all-encompassing. It is not specific to anyone or anything but is the underlying substance and nature of everything.

Energy not only moves through space at the speed of light, it also moves through us and <u>as</u> us. It is the very nature of the body-mind. Particles of light or energy are literally moving through the body in every moment, but we ourselves <u>are</u> energy. The constantly moving and flowing field of energy we call 'ourselves' is continuous with the entire field of energy of the universe.

By engaging in energy practices, such as breath control and the system of circular or rolling movements, and the standing and sitting meditation forms, it becomes possible to actually feel this movement in our own body and to feel this same energy – the vibrant flow of life itself – flowing between each and every being and thing in and around us.

With practice, we can develop a deeper intrinsic sensitivity to touch as a means or access to universal energy. As our feeling of touch deepens (and the mind relaxes), we may begin to feel ourselves as that very living energy within which everything is moving and changing.

Since touch is our natural state, there is nothing to stop us from exploring and discovering it in each moment. Indeed, once you begin exploring intrinsic touch energy in your own life, you will be amazed at how natural, instinctive and right it feels. In the beginning, you just need a bit of help, which is what this book is about. By taking up these exercises, you will find yourself spending more and more time rested in the deeper dimension of intrinsic touch, experiencing life as a living, breathing process and your own bodily form as a touch-body.

The process that is Intrinsic Touch Energy is a practical method that reveals and therefore allows us to enter into this deeper dimension of ourselves and the world we see and feel by observing our capability to receive and feel subtle energy, and to even transmit that healing and rebalancing force to others by recognizing our commonality as universal beings.

Subtle energy can be felt to positively enhance all the body's sense mechanisms, allowing us to magnify a greater degree of love and share the power of our life-force through a deep sensitivity to the subtler realm of intrinsic touch, that is beyond but perfectly attuned to the physical activity of touch.

This book is therefore about process. It is a book about practice rather than theory. You may notice a similarity with exercises from some traditional movement systems, but in this book the exercises are simply a means to help the reader to open more into the feeling dimension. It is not intended to be a comprehensive text about the various theories related to the subtle dimensions of life.

Intrinsic Touch Energy is a tangible and direct connection to the normally invisible energy field known by many names including chi, ki, prana, mana, etheric life-force, and the universal life-force. As the medium for receiving this force, it is implicitly available for the health and rebalancing of the physical body through these various areas of practice:

- circular, flowing, rotating or rolling movements
- conscious deep breathing
- energy testing sensitivity with stillness and movement
- rebalancing sessions with individuals or groups
- energy rebalancing treatments

In the following quote Adi Da offers a simple exercise to explain the nature of energy fields:

"If you rub your hands together, and then hold them close but slightly apart, you can feel the energy between them. You can feel there is a kind of vibratory fluid between the hands. What does that mean? It means that the physical body is not merely "material" in some gross, meat-like sense. The physical body is part of an energy-domain. If you go deeply into the physical dimension, you see it is simply energies. It is mainly space. When you get down to the atomic level, there is a lot of space in between so-called "particles". It is a field of energy. The particles are not particles—when seen truly, they are energy-fields. Everything is energy-fields—everything! There is no "matter".

There is only energy-fields. Everything is an apparition of energy-fields. Everything cosmic, everything conditional, is energy only. There is no matter otherwise. What appears to be matter is a mode of energy. If you get close enough to it, you find matter to be energy. If you get more of a distant view, you feel it as "stuff". But, in truth, there is no "stuff"— there are only fields of energy. Functioning on the basis of this understanding is fundamental human responsibility."

Adi Da Samraj – Conductivity Healing

How to Use This Book

This book can be used in many ways:

- to support general health and well being
- to restore and rebalance energy to the state of the whole body
- to allow the body to enter into a deeper space of conscious feeling
- to allow conscious feeling to be noticed as a profound state of awareness and subtle touch
- to recognise conscious feeling, awareness and subtle touch as our natural state of happiness within all our relationships
- as a life-transformative and intuitive consciously-felt process

Therefore, to get the most out of this book, first read it slowly all the way through to absorb (and visualise) the various exercises and principles outlined throughout the text, including those offered in poetic form.

Then read it again and slowly introduce yourself to the exercises outlined by doing them step by step, bringing care and attention to the subtle details. The exercises can be done to suit your own level of participation. The best way initially is to practice everything slowly, pleasurably and consciously.

The movements can be practised randomly and completely out of the context of a strict routine. The main point here is to find out what benefits you the most by experimenting with them.

Whichever method you choose, always bring great focus through your attention and feeling when performing the movements. Your body may adapt quickly or slowly, there really is no rush at all.

You may find that you come up against your own habitual movement patterns. If so, just relax and continue and you will find these obstructions will gradually release over time as you develop greater body awareness.

As you develop a pattern of energy flow, you will begin to feel your body loosening up and becoming accustomed to the flow of each form of movement.

The purpose of the outline is to adapt to the practices in four stages, although this is not a fixed rule.

The four stages are as follows:

1) Exercise the body using the various loosening practices including swinging, shake out, rotating and flowing movements.
2) Allow the body to relax deeply through exercising the breath combined with the depth of your conscious feeling.
3) Allow your whole bodily sense of conscious feeling to deepen through the practice of stillness.

4) Notice and feel your sensitivity as a conscious feeling of whole bodily awareness.

Such practices as body rolling and flowing movements are simple to do and many can be done even while sitting at a desk, on a train, in a garden or in any free moment, even for a few minutes.

The conscious breathing and stillness exercises require a quiet space ordinarily, but what is also interesting is to feel stillness and calm within a hectic energetic and cluttered environment. A sign of one's deepening practice is to find composure and balance even under such intensive circumstances.

In the fourth stage, the conscious feeling of awareness may be spontaneously noticed at any point throughout these practices. It is not a specific practice as such but a process that arises out of this deepening sense and depth of your awareness.

As we become more sensitised to the universal nature of touch we may notice changes occurring within our relationships with loved ones, the natural environment, and even all beings, places and things.

Therefore, feel and allow yourself to enter into this process as an exploration in the art of "conscious touch", the space that is Intrinsic Touch Energy.

PART 1
Movement

The role our hands play every day
through toil and leisure
through pain through pleasure
Working always from
hands that shake
to hands that give
to hands that take
These hands are more
than what they seem
More than
tool makers
Than artisan creators
Than a masseur's touch
Than refined artistic design
That puts pen to paper
Fingertips to keyboards

What they juggle every day
every hand in every way
They allow a depth
They feel so much
Feel, feel the deepest touch

That touch is
more than skin deep
More than where tears weep
More to feel intrinsically
Beyond the molecular
The atomic, the cellular
Deeper still the touch
feel happens
In the midst
the feeling takes you deep
Deeper than sleep
Sublimed beyond mind
Beyond time

Beyond the reference
Identified
to another place
another zone

There you are centred
There you are washed
There you are held
There you are touch

You are the place
of feeling deep
in the light

Warm
Up
Exercises

S wing into life – with some simple warm up exercises Swinging from left to right then right to left is a natural way to keep the body limber yet strong, taut but loose, focused yet calm, balanced yet energised.

Start from the neutral standing position by first swinging to the right, pivot on the heel of the right foot to support your swing, relax the arms, shoulders and upper body, then swing to the left, pivot on the heel of the left foot to support your swing.

Allow your arms to be very limber as they swing around your body.

Swing for 2–5 minutes. Stand in the neutral standing pose after swinging, feel and allow your

energy to expand outward from the heart centre to all around the body and beyond in preparation for the next exercise.

Conscious shake out

Shake loose from all the binding energies of life. Allow all of the stresses and frustrations to fall away with this benignly simple yet energising and loosening-up exercise.

Stand with knees slightly bent. Lift your arms so they are parallel to each other from the elbow. Drop the hands so they are completely relaxed.

Now rock the knees forward so that your body begins to move vertically up and down. Allow the hands to naturally shake out from the wrists so that as your knees move forward your hands naturally swing downwards.

Practice this motion until you feel a smooth rhythm between your knees motioning forward and back in sync with your hands shaking out easefully and without using any extraneous force.

Keep your back straight with your attention looking forward while remaining focused in the exercise. Practice for 2–5 minutes until you feel relaxed. Exercise your capacity to feel from your heart centre outward throughout the body's sphere and scope.

Note: To radiate your love from the heart out to the world and the universe is a particular sensory feeling practice that can be done in relation to all of these exercises.

The System of Circular or Rolling Movements

The following exercises offer a means to open up the body with particular focus on the joints as follows:

Fingers

Hands

Wrists

Elbows

Shoulders

Neck

Torso

Waist

Hips

Knees

Ankles

Feet

Whole body frontal / spinal line

These simple exercises offer easeful ways to allow the whole body to relax into and be more available for conducting the natural life energy.

Moving the joints through these methods can also help to alleviate stiffness or patterns of blocked energy but more importantly, when the movements are done slowly they allow the body to fall into the space of resonant feeling (or rebalance) and thus deepen our sensitivity to touch as energy presence.

T he **fingers** are flexible and the joints can be exercised using rolling circular motions. Spread your fingers apart and begin by rolling each one and see how it feels.

What do you notice when you do this action?

Are your fingers stiff, loose, strong, weak, flexible, or do they ache?

This may feel a bit like oiling the wheels if you have never tried it before.

Does this movement affect how your whole body feels to some or any degree?

Doing this subtle movement can have the effect of bringing the whole body into a state of relaxation. Set aside the time to do this and see what you discover.

O ur **hands** play such an important role in all of our day-to-day activities but as we're continually using our hands, how often do we exercise them for relief and pleasure?

We can bring relaxing energy to them by allowing our hands to flow in and out using a natural flowing motion, first flowing out as depicted in the images below, with the sense as if water is passing through and out of your hand or even perceiving your hands as literally being water.

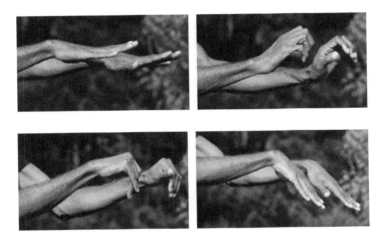

Hold your hands out and see if you can simulate the movement of a jellyfish or sea anemone by exercising all the knuckles with these movements.

Can you feel fluidity in the motion? Are your hands more fluid or stiff?

Now try this movement with the sense of water flowing in through your hands as in the images below, to move in more of a fluid inward motion to simulate bringing energy in through your hands. Think of the movement like a sea of dolphins jumping up and out of the ocean.

It will take a little practice; see if you notice a change in the feeling of your hands once you have gained some fluidity with these hand flexibility movements.

You may even notice a sense of bodily lightness and a literal feeling of energy flowing in and out of your hands.

Practice this exercise as a warm-up for your hands before, during and after using them to do strenuous or rigorous activities.

Allow yourself to feel what this motion brings, not only to your hands but even to your whole body.

Be "Fluidity in Motion".

Our hands, our feet
a living connection
as we feel with all our parts
from top to bottom
head to toe
as energy flow

We are like a battery of sorts
wired to the infinite
tapped into what is
immeasurable and great
a link like a current
of electric juice
subtle in nature
food to the heart, body,
brain and breath

The living of life is
dependent on its source
which is much more
than sustenance
of water, food,
money and sex energy

There is a living energy
touching us
ever deeper
at the core

as the feeling being
mindless, move-less, free

We are that living energy
that living source
and more in its
subtle elevation
we reverberate in it
in tune as it
as feeling beings
of gentle skin and touch
Like tentacles
responding to the
all surrounding light
that is the aura
that we are
in subtle form
intuitively bright

The **wrists** we turn and twist or indeed we should to gain more accessibility and thus to feel the sensation that supports the flowing dynamic force of life that lives within and passes through all our bodily parts. Allow the wrist to hang and without too much effort roll them around in circles, clockwise then anti-clockwise to feel the flexibility that is there. Do you have mobility there?

You may find that by bringing your awareness to an area that feels immobile or blocked will actually help to release it.

 Explore the wrist rotation movement freely, or try it with the hands held flat to gain more of a subtle rotation, then try the full wrist-roll as above but with the hands held naturally.

Explore the roll with both hands held up together, enter into this movement with an easefulness and strength, feel the subtlety and power in the movements while allowing your hands, wrists and arms to release any tension or built-up stress.

Try this for a few moments allowing the wrist, hands and arms to fully relax. Do you notice any difference?

L et go of the need to know
simply engage in the feeling
the release, the allowing
the sense of embracing
freely playing
with everything moving
lose yourself in the fluid movement
feel what the essence is saying
listen to the play of it
the freedom in it
the openness of heart
that brings joy to every cell
fall into that and laugh or cry
with happiness and ecstasy
in your freedom dance of life

F eel the shape of the **elbow** and what it represents to you by putting one hand under your elbow then move your arm forwards and backwards in the action of a pump. Is there flexibility there?

Now go from there to rotating your forearm at the elbow, first clockwise then anti-clockwise. Feel into the effects of this movement. Is it relaxing?

Are your joints stiff, flexible or do they creak a bit?

This area of the body can tend to miss out on mobility and again we can bring awareness to this part of the body and the very act of doing that will help to release degrees of tension.

 Play with this exercise and see if you can rotate both the arms from the elbow at the same time to create a windmill effect with both arms rotating in opposite directions.

The key is to hold the elbows in the same position while rotating both the arms. This may feel awkward at first. If it does, try it like this: Hold both arms up and rotate the left arm once then rotate the right arm once, do this until you can feel how the movement will work naturally one after the other until you get the sense of how they can rotate in unison together.

Now try the rotation with both arms moving in opposite directions, allow the flow of the movement to become like a dance, enjoy it.

Stand tall even if you're small
Think big, really big
Feel beyond yourself
Whoever that is

Presume no limits
no sense of time
Everything is big
Everything is small

Everything is not what it seems at all
Be so happy that you don't care
about shape or size
or measurements of any kind
Simply unwind

Rotate in the sublimity
of all that is!

Shoulders are forever uptight in many ways, in language there are heavy weights to carry or heavy blame laid upon them. We can hunch in a crunch because the weight is too much or sometimes it feels right to be uptight in an odd sort of way, to bear the brunt of whatever weight we may be carrying, tolerating or debating, it's frustrating, shoulders know this only too well.

Therefore we need to unwind this built-up tension we may be holding, in an obvious knowing or unknowing way. Shoulders...you need to relax!

uptight   feeling right

By giving a gentle role to our shoulders regularly, easefully and gracefully, the rotating of our shoulders can serve to relax the whole body and mind.

In this sequence we can easefully role the shoulders forwards then backwards, even while sitting and typing a manuscript or any other action. Remember to keep the back straight easefully, the shoulders relaxed as your breathing cycle remains both deep and calm.

How does it feel
when you do that action?
Are you loose?
Are you stiff?
Are you strong?
Are you flexible?
Do you creak
like an armchair?
Do you need oiling?

Do your wheels need turning?
Does the movement affect how you feel?
Can you feel subtly?
Did you relax freely?
Now, how do you feel?

Tension can appear everywhere in the body, especially as we mature in age. The old adage of our "age catching up on us" can feel most apt, however, even in younger folks. All kinds of tensions can appear for any number of reasons.

Our **necks** know this only too well which is why it's important to keep the neck as with the shoulders exercised regularly. Don't wait to get uptight, we should be prepared to deal with these tensions whether we're feeling them or not, as it is guaranteed that the body will be dealing with various stresses whether in early or later life. We need to unwind these knots…right now!

The neck roll can be done gently in two alternate ways to get maximum relaxation. Either by lowering your head forward and rotating the head fully by making a wide circle taking the lead from the top of the head or the head can be rotated with less movement in the neck to make a smaller circular gentle rotation.

These two types of rotations feel slightly different. See if you can notice the difference.

Does one movement feel more beneficial than the other? Or are both good?

Experiment with these especially if you're feeling under pressure, a bit run down, suffering from a headache or feeling mentally stressed out.

See if these rotating movements make a difference. Remember to relax into the movements easefully while allowing thought patterns to drift into the background.

How do we simply allow the flow
How do we cease to know
How can we be without knowing
How do we know not to know
How do we allow the flowing

Can we know the unknown without knowing
Can the known be unknown without flowing
Can we flower at night
be bright in the day
Can a cat be uptight
Can a dog lose its way

Can a deer be alert
and still be at play
Can a fox be so cunning
while he is running

Can a skunk not spray
can a snake not hiss
can a whale be heard and not seen
Can the sea 'see' where the whale has been

Can the sun shine
Does it, all the time
Can the wind blow
Can lightning strike
Can the thunder crack

Well…it might
Or rumble and tumble
and role as mountains crumble
in rivers of heat, red and white

A mountain can flow
A body can know
A heart can feel
A baby can die
A life is lived

So, we ask why?
But we don't know
We just don't know
That is the way
the flow

A

rm Stretch / Torso Roll

Stretching the **arms** and rotating the **torso** is a good way to feel the whole body's participation as a living energy dynamic. The rotation can be exercised to suit your degree of natural flexibility while also allowing the body to fall into the rhythm of the rotation.

Feel into the stretch positions as you rotate from the waist. Feel and allow the body to open up as you stretch and rotate in a smooth motion. With the arms stretched upward, feel the extension from your shoulders without overstretching and lean into the exercise in a graceful and easeful manner.

Lean to the left then rotate forward to the right then lean backwards as you rotate with arms stretched. Bend your knees to give more support and even rotate the torso in a larger circle of movement.

Start with eight rotations in each direction, first clockwise then anti-clockwise. Increase the rotations as your body becomes more flexible while being mindful not to overstretch your arms, shoulders and/or lower back.

Stand for a few moments after finishing the exercise and feel your whole body's natural state of balance and participation within the environment from the inside out.

Breathe into and feel the whole body deeply and consciously before continuing with the routine.

R olling the **hips** and exercising the waist is fun and very simple to do by shifting the body around while keeping the torso straight. First shift your hip to the left, then shift to the front, then shift to the right, then shift your rear end back, then straighten up and repeat until you can feel a rolling action in one sequence of movement.

This exercise is very danceable due to the rolling movements and can be practised while listening to music that you enjoy. I recommend soft calming music for relaxation or upbeat music with nice percussion sounds for uplifting energy.

oving love
Moving touch
Moving little
Moving much

Moving with
Moving by
Moving slowly
Moving high

Moving power
Moving force
Moving flower
Moving source
Moving face
Moving smile

Moving senses
Moving style
Moving now
Moving then
Moving some
Moving all

Moving sisters
Moving brothers
Moving fathers
Moving mothers
Moving lover
Moving lovers

Moving space
Moving time
Moving grace
Moving sign
Moving free

oving is
heart
ecstasy

So
Move

This more technical version of the **hip** roll lends itself to the movements found in dance forms such as Hawaiian hula or traditional Middle Eastern belly dancing. In the first position, crouch slightly while standing as if resting your rear end on a stool, keeping the feet parallel and close together.

Swing the hips to the left, then shift the hip forward, then swing to the right, then shift your rear end back. Repeat the movement until you begin to feel you're loose enough to continue the action in one fluid rotating, rolling movement.

Reverse the movement by swinging the hips to the right, then forward, then to the left, then back as above.

I recommend watching some belly or hula dancing, which will give you a better feel for how the movement physically works and also add to your dance repertoire.

This rotation movement loosens up the hip joints and is therefore beneficial to the body as we mature in age. Many people suffer from fractures in the hips as they grow older which can lead to hip replacements. This exercise helps to keep your hips supple and strong and also keeps the body youthful – energetically and sexually.

This is also useful for maintaining a natural youthfulness and strength throughout the whole body and particularly the energy associated with the lower body.

The Cat

The cat is agile, supple
Moves with dexterity
with all of energy
equanimity and poise
Its lightness is a surprise
whiskers, swirling tail
cannot fail to delight
Awaiting, flexing, shaping
attentive, smart, alert
inert, twitching ear
calm, rested, fluid
perky, unrepressed
perfectly balanced
all purring, exploring
with deft insight
inclined in its nature
to be just as it is

The **knee** roll, as with many of these rotational movements, is associated with the ancient practices of qigong and tai chi. It helps to maintain the natural suppleness in the knees, especially to counter old age and the wearing down of muscle tissue, muscle tendons and bone structure.

Traditionally these movements are best performed slowly to allow for better reception of energy flow throughout the whole body.

Bend the knees, keeping both knees and feet together with both hands on the knees. Shift the knees to the right using the hands as support, then back, then to the left, then to the front to create a smooth rotation. Keep the back straight throughout the exercise.

Reverse the roll starting by shifting to the left, then back, then to the right then forward while maintaining a smooth rotation.

K nee and **ankle** roll

This exercise serves both balance and flexibility of the legs with a particular focus on the knee joints.

Stand with feet shoulder width apart, bend your knees slightly then raise your left leg so that your raised leg is up at a 90-degree angle from your standing leg. Keep your left hand on the knee to support your balance.

Rotate your calf clockwise for eight rotations then anti-clockwise for eight rotations.

Lower your knee slightly and rotate your ankles for eight rotations clockwise then eight rotations anti-clockwise. Loosen the joints in your feet by bending them forwards then backwards including the toe joints.

Flex your feet in different directions to gain more

stretch and flexibility. Now repeat the sequence with your right leg.

If you find standing on one leg awkward at first, try using a chair or sidebar to keep your balance until you feel strong enough to do the exercise without any additional support.

Alternatively, you can do both of these exercises while lying flat on a mat. Raise your leg from the lying down position to a 90-degree angle and do the rotations as you would while standing.

The ankle rotations can also be practised while sitting on a chair or bench.

The **ankle** roll – Sitting

Sit in a supportive chair with your back straight. Point the left toe forward and roll the ankle around in circular motions, then reverse the motion. Bend the toes back slightly to stretch the joints and musculature of the feet. Moving the ankle in large circles, point the toes downwards at the lowest point of the circle and then bend them back as you reach the higher part of the circle. Repeat the exercise with the right foot. (You can also try pointing both feet forward and rolling both ankles in opposite directions).

This sense of touch
is lightning fast
Time-less, space-less
green as grass
Just as the sun sees everyone
already spun
touch is the sun
weaved into every fabric
of physical design
that feels alive
and moves around
as a life sign
whether a still tree
a flower in the wind
a rain shower
or the tiniest
of living invisibility
that no naked eye can see
touch is intertwined intrinsically

Touch is open access
readily available, flexible
likeable
loveable
implausible
uncaused
unphased

unshaken

without shape or size

eternally wise

A dvanced standing **ankle/feet** roll while standing, rolling on both feet at the same time.

Stand with your feet together. Feel your connection to the ground, and how your feet are weighted into the ground.

Bend the knees as if you are about to do the knee rolling exercise while keeping the body upright with your arms to your side, then press the knees together. Rotate the knees together in a clockwise motion (the same way you rotate them in the knee roll). As you rotate, remain upright with your hands by your sides.

Bend the knees Roll to right of the feet then the front of the feet

ontrol the pace and balance of the roll by pressing the knees firmly together. As you roll the knees, try and concentrate on the movement of the balls of the feet. Roll around in a full circle, shifting your weight slightly.

You should be able to feel the sides of the feet rolling around on the floor. Roll in small circles so you don't lose balance.

Then to the left of the feet   Then back on the heels

Fingers
Hands
Wrists
Arms
Shoulders
Neck
Chest
Torso
Waist
Hips
Thighs
Knees
Ankles
Feet
All refreshed
Regenerated
Revitalised
Opened to receive
Touch Energy
Intrinsically
Rolled, rotated
A whole body feeling
Sense of aura bathed
A calmed mind creates
an open space
A softened heart

prepares for grace

To enter into silence

Still as body

Soothing calm

This tranquil place

fills full the need

At heart

Of seedlings flower born

from underground

to crack the Earth

and feel the light abound

Your newly flowered

personhood

Serenity in peace

can flower ever wider

Arms stretching

like trees

Fingers sensitised

to a gentle breeze

This body is the tree

The homeland

of an inner sea

Where the blood

flows like rivers

the cells swim

the body quivers

as life shivers
through it
Electrically
Magnetically
Spontaneously
Beautifully
Completely

F rontal/spinal energy flow

This movement can be combined with conscious breathing by syncing the breath with the flow of the movement.

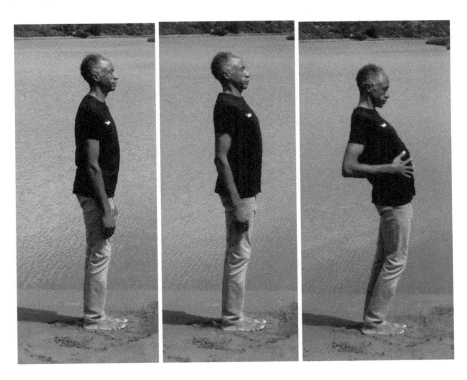

Standing in an upright position breathe in as you raise the chest up then allow the breath to move down into the abdominal region while allowing the mid-section of your body to naturally fold in and down to the hips which should roll back slightly. Now reverse the movement with the out-breath.

Swing the hips forward as you breathe out, move the mid-section with the flow of breath, bringing the chest out as you breathe out and return to an upright position.

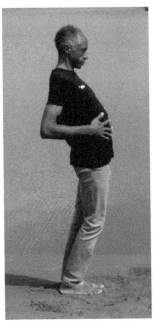

You can also try the movement without focusing on the breath. Once you feel more mobile and fluid, the flow of breath with movement should feel natural and easeful. This movement is very much associated with water and the movement of water in and as our bodies.

It also reminds us that the body is primarily comprised of water, as much as 75%.

Therefore, recognise that your body is more of an elemental water form and is by no means or in any sense fixed. It is a bio-molecular form that will eventually dissolve. However, we inhere in a dimension that is so much more than that.

It is a matter of discovering the depth of who and what we really are through entering more profoundly into the mysteries of existence by exploring our sense of space as touch.

PART 2
Breath

E motions
Do emotions run high in life?
Sometimes I think they do
We may feel out of touch
with our body's sensory mechanism
Suppressing it
Expressing it
Stressfully, mentally, physically
To the point of overload
Yes!
We can explode
when we're out of touch
Or implode when to touch
just seems too much

So we can hide
Stay inside of our
emotional fears
Express outrage
pain, be lost in tears

Always through every drama
we can be calmer

we can engage the

breath of life

In every cycle breathed

down abdominally deep

the energy a secret charmer

will quietly creep

It will mingle

It will tingle

With every body part

From head to toe

You see, not at all fixed

is complete transparency

So, breathe through it

The sorrow

The fear

The anger

Know it again

But breathe deeper still

Allow if you will

this entrance

this repentance

To be quiet

To be still

Breathe and know

that we live above

and not below

This body form
is only one part
We can grow
and be
esoterically high

The physical body and breathing dimensions are what we're most aware of biologically and physiologically, with such processes as the natural senses that stimulate a multitude of sensory responses via the brain and central nervous system.

In any moment whether we're active or inactive we can choose to take a moment to breathe and feel the subtler energy dimension. We can breathe the natural life-force into the navel and feel a universal presence.

As you engage breathing as a practice, follow these general guidelines: Breathe in and out through the nose. Press the tongue slightly against the pallet of the mouth just behind the teeth, this will help to support your ability to feel and conduct the natural life-energy.

Exercise.1 Take a moment right now for 1–2 minutes to observe and feel the nature of your breathing.

Breathing as a natural cycle is a vastly integrated process that may at first seem to be just a matter of breathing oxygen in and out of the lungs.

However, upon closer inspection, we may notice that the breath not only brings oxygen into and through the body but it actually conducts subtle life-energies throughout the body's entire feeling structure.

The body and breath is a holistic-feeling energy dynamic and when we allow the breath to be felt more subtly by relaxing into the space of our breathing, we may notice the breath as life-force itself. The breathing of life-force is actually the feeling of universal presence.

Exercise.2 Take a moment now to consider your breathing:

Are you the one really doing the breathing? Is there something you have to think about or engage in before breathing occurs? Or is your breathing occurring spontaneously?

If you're not doing the breathing or making it consciously happen, what is your relationship to breathing? Allow your whole being to feel into the nature of your breathing as a life-replenishing, restorative process.

By taking the time to simply observe the process of our breathing and its overall effect on our total structure as a human being, we can consciously engage and feel our breathing as a living and energising process.

Therefore, we can use the breath to fully function by being aware of how to breathe and bring life energy into the total physiological and biological structure of the body.

The following excerpt is a guided meditation exercise from *Drifted in the Deeper Land*, a book by Adi Da Samraj. This exercise focuses explicitly on the breath. Really feel into each line and notice, without becoming fixated on it, the motion of your breathing. Read it slowly. Repeat the exercise as many times as you need to.

Guided breathing/contemplation exercise

Can you feel your heart beat? It is happening.

You're not doing it. So, what are you?

You just are.

You just have to feel into the source of the heartbeat.

And the source of the breath.

Feel where the inhalation begins and where the exhalation begins.

The source of that.

Each breath and each heartbeat.

Just simply feel that.

Where is the breath arising?

Where does the gesture of inhalation begin?

What is the source of it?

You just have to feel it.

Notice how you feel as you do this. What happens to your breath? Does it slow? Does it feel deeper?

Contained within this excerpt is a profound consideration about the breath and being itself: the importance of feeling where the breath comes from. The origin of the breath, as intimated in this passage, is a mystery to simply be rested in.

Energy works subtly
unknown, known
creative essence
mysterious presence
heart sensitive touch
feeling depth
thoughtless intuition
letting the body go
as if falling, no fear
falling out of mind
into the heart place
a field of pleasure
replenished
bathed in conscious light
the body given over
selflessly, effort free
trusting the mystery
allowing without knowing
not knowing is the key
this happiness is flowing
you release the knowing
the 'you' cannot know
what the heart is
be the touch
presence

At the dimension of feeling, we live as a bodily process of expansion and contraction when faced with outward and objective or inward and subjective feelings in response to our life circumstances. The heart is a mechanism in nature when felt from the core as a place of raw feeling. The physical heart is a very vulnerable part of our biological structure, as any of our internal organs are, but with regard to the dimension of feeling, the heart and total area around the chest and throat represents a special vulnerability that relates to feeling and self-expression.

Exercise.3 Heart vulnerability exercise

- *Stand with the body upright or sit in a comfortable posture with the back loose and straight and legs crossed at the ankles to support conductivity of the natural life-energy*
- *Place both of your hands over your heart, left over right, close your eyes and take the time to listen and feel your heart beating*
- *Feel into its utter vulnerability and dependency on the breath and the life-force to maintain its cycle*
- *As you breathe, try to focus your breath in the lower body*
- *Feel how the breath and the heartbeat are utterly dependent upon each other*
- *Rest in this deep space of vulnerability for a few moments until you're ready to continue reading*

Whenever we feel shut down, even if the physical body appears to be in good health and our mental faculties are functioning normally, we still may be unaware of collapsed energy at the heart and core of our being. To feel from our human hearts is not a common practice, though in general as a human race we do strive to improve and grow in all areas of life.

The heart, however, has a greater capacity for love and depth of feeling which stretches beyond what we may at first be aware of at the level of human relationships and love for our fellow beings.

The secret of "conductivity": Treat or relate to the phenomenal "world" and "self" (or the body-mind complex) as energy rather than mere matter. And treat or relate to every condition of the phenomenal "world" and "self"— positive or negative, high or low—as the same Ultimate and Total Energy (or Self-Radiance of Transcendental Spiritual Divine Being. Body and mind are the same energy. Use every condition or circumstance as an incident of transmission of energy, continuous with the Radiant Principle of Divine Being. Open to energy, contact it, and circulate it. And communicate it in all directions and relations through love.

Adi Da Samraj –Conductivity Healing

This depth of love is active at a subtler level of our awareness, deeper than any emotional expression of heart intimacy and companionship. At its core, love is a doorway to our life in ecstasy as consciousness, thus to enter into this place of in-depth feeling is a most profound matter.

Intrinsic Touch Energy begins at the heart as vulnerability and deep silence.

This deep silence of your heart's awareness has great strength. Therefore, feel your stance as this balance and state of equanimity as you begin the next exercise.

Exercise. 4 Repeat the heart vulnerability exercise below

This time allow your whole body to be in the mode of energy reception and energy release via the breath.

Feel the whole body in relationship to your heartbeat.

Feel what is occurring within the body as you breathe deeply and rest in this space of feeling from your heart.

When you're ready, open your eyes, stand and take three full breaths.

Breathe deeply in and out in the mode of reception of energy and release of energy before you continue reading.

By allowing our whole body to feel from its core to that which extends beyond it, we can feel that which is infinitely wide and without limit.

When the heart is awakened to consciousness as pure feeling, we are as if reborn into another depth and world of love that is profoundly liberating and is our natural state.

Ex.5 Energy expansion via the heart – How to radiate your love in all directions

This practice allows the body to drop into the sensory space of feeling as energy expansion by extending the sense of our love beyond our physical sphere.

What is that sphere? Are we only bound in and as a physical body limited to skin, flesh and blood? Are we some kind of walking structured thing that has no other capability to feel more than its physical appearance as an apparent separate self?

By relaxing the frontal line and chest area of the body and by feeling our connection to the earth from head to toe, we may notice that we're able to stand up vertically not only as a by-product of gravity but we're also wired into the energy field of our surroundings, magnetically and literally as energy receptors and connectors.

We can truly test what we are as energy by deepening our sensitivity to our surroundings by feeling from inside to outside from our hearts. This allows us to notice that the heart has the capacity to radiate energy through the feeling of love and intimate touch. In other words, we can feel spherically as an energy body.

When exercised consistently and felt into as the space of love, we can literally notice the heart as naturally living in a spherical space during this process without any effort.

The following exercises in the 'Stillness' section will allow the body to begin to open out naturally, to notice more the sensory feeling and spherical space of intrinsic touch.

PART 3
Stillness

Feel your heart beat

With flow of breath

Listen in the silence

All around

A shimmering

of soundless sound

of life

of heart

of everything

I t may seem obvious to say that by coming together we can make a difference but making a difference that has a profound transformative effect at the centre of our lives is perhaps one of the greatest challenges we face as a species.

Finding a commonality that brings people together in many areas of our lives is interesting to consider, as the basis of people coming together is usually centred on shared feelings of unity that corresponds with the depth of our feeling energy.

When we "click" in a moment with an individual or group, the nature of our being begins to register something that may not be explainable in the usual sense of our responsive faculties. Such moments can indicate a link we may share that is operative in moments of sudden and spontaneous openings that register at the place of our subtle awareness.

Togetherness is a homogenous feeling, a literal feeling of being a part of, or belonging to, a source which connects all parties to feel their place and link to that source. The source can be anything, and people can come together for: good, bad and positive or negative reasons.

The key to togetherness is harmony and the feeling of energy balance, such that we are somehow residing in a shared energy field that takes everything into account including all the personal and collective needs that reflect the full summation of the whole.

Let's consider this sense of harmony through the practice of feeling an awareness and natural sensitivity to our surroundings with the practice of breathing and feeling from the inside to out.

Exercise.5 The Practice of Stillness

Try this "pressing hands" exercise preferably in a quiet place surrounded by natural beauty, trees, rocks, etc. or find a set-apart place with benign energy.

- Begin by taking five deep breaths into the navel while sitting or standing.
- Breathe deeply until you're fully relaxed.
- Be aware of your posture by keeping your back straight and supple whether sitting or standing.

- Now bring your hands and arms up by moving your arms from the elbows with the palms facing upwards. (see fig. 1)
- Move your arms from the elbow while breathing into your lower body as you move the forearms up to the body's mid-section.

fig. 1   *fig. 2*

- *Now turn the palms facing downwards and breathe out.*
- *(see fig. 2)*
- *Feel from the centre of your palms while breathing in and out.*
- *Repeat the hand/arm motion with the in-breath and out-breath for ten movements.*
- *Breathe in, hands move up.*
- *Breathe out, hands move down.*

- *Now relax and consider your place of stillness where the whole body can feel its surroundings.*
- *Feel your heart and whole body's connection to the natural environment as living energy while remaining still.*
- *Fully breathe and feel into the space while remaining completely relaxed.*

Now affirm either silently or vocally with these words from your heart:

I AM AS ONE WITH THE UNIVERSE AND ALL THAT SURROUNDS ME

MY HEART RESTS IN THE DEEP SILENT SPACE OF INTRINSIC CALM

- Repeat these affirmations several times until it is felt as a strong force of conviction from your heart.
- Try the affirmations either with your eyes open or closed
- Surrender deeply into the environment and simply feel your connection with everything.
- You may find you have sensitivity to the vibratory nature of your surroundings. Simply allow this to be so.
- Even if you do not feel any particular form of sensitivity, do not be concerned.
- Even without that sensitivity, you have entered into a connection with your surroundings which will mature and grow with practice.

The body is energy:

An aspect of it appears to be solid, but it is only a certain frequency of vibration.

There exist many higher and many lower vibration of the being.

Beyond a certain point in this great spectrum of vibrations, you lose the "visibility" of the Divine Reality, you lose track of the Depth of Infinity-because your physical stress attunes you only to this limited vibration of apparent matter.

But, if that stress relaxes, you can feel that the physical body and energy are the same.

Can you feel that the body is only free energy-right now?

You can feel a tension, an urge to want to hold something in your heart.

But that is just your stress, your reluctance to relax, your suppression of Radiance, of Love, of profuse Happiness.

Let that contraction go, and you will feel the whole body radiate.

Adi Da Samraj — The Body is Energy, Conductivity Healing

B reathing, feeling
as we are
as feeling touch
sensory space
Abound

Thoughtless divine
Timeless sign we are

In this space of breathing
listen with serenity
of heart

As responsive being
every cell is feeling
We are feeling
all around literally
through communion
with the Source
This sensory space
is always full, alive
Bright Ecstatic
Always Now

We are sensory beings
made to feel through
windowless time
We are timeless beings

made intrinsically
We are Epiphany

Every particle unbound
alive in this
as touch
as love
as heart
as One
as timeless
soundless sound

In this sensory mode
touch the fingertips together

Eyes open or closed
Either sitting or standing

With a slight pressure
press the fingertips together

Allow this touch sensory mode
Felt from heart to hand
to fingertips

Allow the breath
to be deep in then out
Cyclically, lower bodily

Feeling deeply in this
touch sensory dimension

Feel the depth
the sense of whole bodily self

Do you notice the sense of
whole bodily self as touch?
Explore your feeling connection
in this manner for a while

In every being there is a power
Like earth, like dirt
Like fire-blown glass
Like clay pots heated
within a kiln

Like a school of wild fish
thrashing through waves
that crash in, up and down
like the deepest sound
heard from miles around

A whale, a lion's roar
a large seashell
blown in trumpets blare
of bugle-playing days
in wars untold

We fold in and out
from past to present
yet in time we yield
to our mortality

By grace
our true heart rests
beyond the sea
ignited uproariously
beyond the dirt splattered
sounds of underground

Of heated chambers
ashen pot
in past history
we are not that
and never were
or could ever be

This power is
beyond all of that

PART 4
Awareness

The fourth dimension of Intrinsic Touch Energy occurs through the deepening of our Intuitive Conscious Awareness, which is not something we can conjure up through some form of technique.

A deepening of our sensitivity to energy as feeling reveals how we are already free participants in the energy field of awareness. While awareness is not an action as such, awareness can be noticed as our natural state wherein we are more sensitised to life as an intuitive energy process.

In other words, we are not doing awareness, we are already intuitively aware of being connected to everyone and everything as awareness. Therefore, by entering into a space of deep stillness, we may notice something unique about our relationship to everyone and everything.

By getting out of the way of any emotional impact we may have on or toward another, or toward anything at all, we can feel what is deeper and more profound than our emotional influence.

There is no reaction in the space of awareness, therefore being consciously aware allows our heart to be present as feeling, love and happiness.

There is no specific exercise than to simply allow our whole body, heart and mind to notice that is what and who we are, without identity, influence, name tag, culture or any kind of predisposition of association even to form or structure.

Awareness as an intuitive feeling is unencumbered by any such influence and knows no bounds or limitations in the moment of allowing and being as awareness is.

This happy space of intrinsic touch energy releases us from fear, pain, negativity, attachment and the struggles we associate with our usual patterned life. It is not an escape from our patterned lives but more of an embrace of the profound depth and fullness of life felt from and as the heart of being itself. This profundity is the feeling of joy, love-touch-happiness, from and as the heart, the reality space of what and who we really are.

It is imperative that we allow our minds and whole body to drop into the reality of what and who we really are by entering more profoundly into the feeling of love itself.

This love is immeasurable and unlimited whenever we allow our hearts to enter into this limitless space of free feeling. To allow this moment to be truly entered into requires the entire being to see and feel beyond the usual constraints of fear, doubt and uncertainty we may be troubled by. Even in the midst of any and all emotional, physical, mental or psychological constraints, the feeling of love itself exists already and is always available.

To truly understand this, we must have a deep faith in our hearts that this is so. The processes described in this book are a support to our deep faith.

How do we find such deep faith? Everyone has this same potential to know such deep faith by intuitively inspecting the nature of reality, and through feeling what reality really is as a living process.

Beyond the states of mind and body, deeper than the breath and heartbeat, there is a purity of unencumbered feeling and subtle radiance. By allowing our heart to rest in this purity of being, we may feel a brightness that shines from there, regardless of any disturbances and distractions of mind and psyche, or any physical restrictions including physical pain, and the body as a whole can be surrendered into this place of purity and being.

To feel from the inside out is to feel from this deep space of natural calm which is unperturbed and radiant. True faith is a personal feeling, a gift that allows the heart to be released into a greater depth of serenity, peace and radiance.

We do not own our lives from the perspective of grace, our lives are returned to the heart, returned to a state of balanced wholeness, love and freedom, giving us a greater capability to deal with our lives in the midst of whatever limitations we may feel.

The true heart _is_ always free and full of bright happiness.

The true heart _is_ the purity of being itself.

The true heart _is_ infinite love.

Sensory Awareness Exercise

This exercise is an illuminating way to enter into the deep space of our awareness by considering what and who we really are.

Read the following sections slowly, pausing between each line of question. Breathe slowly and consciously throughout the exercise.

Feel into these questions without looking for an answer.

1) What are you as a body, feeling, mind and breath?

2) What are you in terms of thinking and brainwave patterning?

3) What are you as memory and identity?

4) What are you as objective and subjective perception?

5) What are you as a physical structure, as skin tissue, flesh, bone and muscle?

6) What are you as biological organs, as a brain, heart, lungs, liver, kidneys, intestines, bladder and genitals?

7) What are you as blood vessels, blood, water and liquid?

8) What are you as a nervous system, as electronic brain signals, as visual and mental perception?

9) What are you as energy, light and feeling?

10) What are you as a soul, as pure feeling and love?

11) What are you as subtle energy beyond body and mind?

12) What are you as sensory awareness, touch and heart?

13) What are you as conscious awareness?

14) What are you as consciousness without form or identity?

Allow your entire being to feel beyond the conventions of mental knowledge, ego and emotional self-identity.

Allow even more the reality of "not knowing", of sensory feeling and open awareness.

Feel into that and allow your true self to simply be who and what you really are, with no preconceived notion or idea. Simply rest in the absolute efficacy of this self-revealing knowledge.

Be rested in the "not knowing" and recognise and feel something more profound in relationship to existence itself.

Reread or record and replay these questions as many times as you need until you notice a letting go of your identity while entering into the deeper space of your intuitive conscious awareness.

The Choice to Rebalance Your Life

We live in a world where the dimension of feeling is not always magnified fully at the level of sensitivity to "feeling itself" throughout our so-called "ordinary dance" of day-to-day living.

Feeling as non-reactivity, as the impulse, the desire and the passion of the heart is the real and necessary root of our lives, to know love at a deeper and more transformative level.

How does this understanding translate into our real lives....no matter what walk of life that we're all involved with?

Everybody breathes and feels in every activity at the ordinary and even extraordinary levels of experience.

Simply walking around and noticing life itself is the most basic level of awareness and which, when truly felt, can even be seen as extraordinary.

We can relate to our surroundings in an explicitly meaningful way by entering into a depth of sensibility toward everything we do.

Even when we're engaged in the most mundane things, this process can and should be felt as a constant discovery, no matter what we're doing.

Feeling is also spirit, which we can notice tangibly as the zest of life. We may walk around in life like a blinkered horse unable to see fully and completely, cut off from our surroundings, unable to access the full feeling of our lives in spirit.

The beauty is that we do not ever have to live a blinkered life at the mercy of non-feeling; we always have a choice. The choice is both simple and profound. It is to see our lives not as something separate from others, as if these bodies are merely functional things, but instead to recognise the process at the root and source of our existence. It is to enter into the governing principle that brought these forms into being.

To know again that at the heart we are never separate from anyone or anything, ever. We can feel this to be absolutely true, even under all the conditions of life whether positive or negative. Even in the wake of negative circumstances such as the great disasters we're seeing in the world today. These events can serve to bring us closer together in the midst of the fear of losing touch or of being annihilated.

Living in the domain of feeling is our great gift to share with each other, despite the signs of difference and intolerance that we may feel ourselves to be at odds with. Those forms of difference and intolerance are the signs of our contracted and limited feeling.

In some sense human society is in a state of constant disaster and constant turmoil. Eventually everyone must deal with the passing of loved ones and our own passing beyond this life.

Sensitising our heart, mind and body to be attentive in the domain of feeling as we live, grow, change and eventually transform out of this life, prepares us to begin to understand something critically important to our very existence.

What is important to our very existence is that we exist as energy, as life-force, as subtle being, and consciously aware which can never be completely destroyed. Energy only ever changes; molecules are transformed, water evaporates and light particles exist in a sea of all-pervading light.

The deeper understanding of this living process is a lifelong-and-beyond exploration into the depth of consciousness. Therefore, by entering into and embracing this process in an ordinary manner, while feeling the implications of this embrace can lead to seeing life in the context of a far greater reality than we could ever have conceived or imagined.

At its root the reality of consciousness as the source of all feeling is no different than who we are at depth right now. Intrinsic Touch Energy can be seen and felt as a gateway into the deeper dimension of unlimited Feeling Conscious Awareness.

Which is the <u>Heart</u>-<u>Light</u> that <u>is</u> all of us.

PART 5
Conscious Touch

Conscious Touch

What is your life if it is not touch?

Can you feel your life from inside out? How is that even possible?

What moves through all life yet goes unnoticed?

What is touching you now and in every moment from birth to death and beyond?

What is the source of your life and of all of life?

What is touch?

What do you feel touch is?

Do you feel touch _is_?

What is touching everything all at once and always?

Can we be consciously fully aware of this?

Try to touch everything now...can you do it?

If everything is touch then you can or can you not?

The lessons of touch are vast, so can we learn to be aware as touch all the time?

Let us find out if this is so by finding our way consciously in this discovery of conscious touch.

Subtle Energy Treatments

Treating anyone with subtle energy is a very powerful process for both the recipient and the practitioner, in which both may experience a sense of transformation through the reception of the subtle energy.

The way Intrinsic Touch Energy works through any individual is quite profound in that the communication of energy being transmitted works to bring the entire body to rest at a physical, emotional and mental level which may include the release of stuck energy throughout the body's structural and cellular patterning.

The recipient may or may not be aware of these effects or even notice how the energy is working in them until after the treatment is over and they've had time to absorb and notice any changes in how they feel physically, mentally and emotionally.

The energy is such that it can allow the recipient to enter into a deep state of relaxation (or sleep). At the end of the treatment, there may still be an overwhelming desire to rest even more, which is perfectly normal as this means the process is entering into the body's sense of awareness at a deeper level.

As the body relaxes, the energy process works to relieve all tension and pain-related stress including mental, emotional and physical stress, which is reflected through the deepness of the breath as the process is being absorbed throughout the body's nervous system and connecting to its brainwave patterning, its cellular structure, all of its biological organs, its skin surface, and physical structure, including the muscles, tendons and bones.

The brain is allowed to fall into a deeper state of brainwave activity which calms the nervous system intrinsically at a heightened feeling level allowing the recipient to breathe more easefully, to rest into more of a thoughtless and mindless state of equanimity and natural balance.

This state of balance (or rebalance) is such that if the recipient remains sensitive to it and continues to live in such a way as to support this shift in their awareness – for instance, by following the guidelines within this book – then they will gain greater long-term benefit than the immediacy of the initial restorative treatment.

The recipient plays an important part in the process by developing their own sensitivity to touch through relaxing into the mood of receiving subtle and physical touch, allowing the body to be at ease throughout the whole period and beyond.

In many cases, more than one or even several treatments may be needed to allow the body to relax more deeply into a state of natural receptivity of the subtle-force of Intrinsic Touch Energy.

On Energy Blocks

We can address some aspects of energy blocks in the body related to general movement, through exercising the joints or through loosening our muscles to create a suppler flexible platform for energy flow, which is a necessary aspect of this process.

We may even be able to address emotional and mental blocks which can lead to bodily stiffness evidenced as trapped emotional feelings,

or mental and emotional fears that may even cripple our capability to function fully, by learning how to recognise the emotional and mental triggers that are at the root of these states of our emotional and mental reactions.

We may even be able to change the physical state of the body by changing our actions through taking on certain health regimes such as exercising more regularly, eating a more balanced diet, and regulating how and what we eat.

These and many other actions may directly affect the degree of energy flow throughout the whole body, which may result in a more balanced state of health and well-being.

In the process of Intrinsic Touch Energy, we can create greater energy flow by recognising that the body is an energy vehicle that is particularly sensitised to the flow of subtle energy even if we're not fully aware of how subtle energy works.

We may not even notice subtle energy flow at all but rather feel its effects afterwards which can be noticed as the feeling of bodily lightness or simply feeling refreshed and happier. This will happen through being able to enter into the subtler energy field that surrounds our physical body.

In effect, we may still notice stiffness in the joints and other aspects of energy blocks such as emotional and mental constraints but the difference is that our association with these blocks can change by virtue of being "tuned in" to the awareness of that process that is outside of and therefore not affected or limited by our physical, emotional or mental constraints and which may allow these constraints to open up naturally and become less and less noticed over time.

This is a very important aspect of Intrinsic Touch Energy as it means we do not need to focus our energy on undoing blockages of a physical, emotional or mental nature. We should remain focused on the literal transformative process of the subtler dimension that draws us into the deeper state of our natural awareness.

Intrinsic Touch Energy is not about making an effort to undo the knots or blocks we may notice in the body, but rather it's about connecting to that which is already flowing and present prior to the physical body, through what can be called the subtle energy field or etheric body or deeper states of awareness.

The simple exercises outlined in this book are to help the whole bodily system to become more relaxed, attuned and to open up freely and easefully without making any forced effort or wilful action. Everything we do should be done artfully and with great care so the whole body will develop a natural receptivity to this process at the feeling level.

E lemental Being

Walk on grass or concrete
feel the bare feet
in every crevice of earth to touch
locate again the dirt
the bladed leaves
soft underfoot

Stand alone, planted
like a tree, its roots
threaded intermittently
in relation to its fellow beings
feel this knowledge in
ball of feet wisdom

Your tiptoes lightly brushing
the touch greenery
Sensibility is this naked skin
birthed in liquid
slipped out into open space

With new eyes sparkle bright
looking, searching, feeling
an earth-born new being
awakens into a life of feeling

guided in sensations
heart identity

So born, labelled,
Identified
and cradled
made to feel another
separate one
a daughter
a son
to grow in feeling earth
to play in sandy beaches
water washing waves
salted smile, happy
loving youthful energy
the life waves in emotions
shifting subtle potions
of a heart child's innocence

The Elemental and the Subtle

When we combine the elemental with the subtle in a more direct way, we can begin to notice a change in relationship to our body's ability to respond to subtle energy.

By coming into contact with water we can feel immediate refreshment both internally and externally as the body is primarily composed of up to 75% water. The body, therefore, can be considered to be a "water" body.

Submerging the body in the ocean or the sea is a beautiful way to feel into the subtle dimension. Being surrounded by water is the same as being surrounded by energy, and through harmonising with water we can feel how subtle energy moves through water since water is a variable elemental substance (also subtler in nature) that can be turned into steam, ice or heated to high temperatures or be frozen to low temperatures yet still be returned to its original state.

Water has many different qualities of vibration, and one of those qualities is feeling subtle touch vibrations within and as water. Explore this feeling of water sensation whenever you enter into the ocean, sea or environments with natural rivers and waterfalls.

The feeling of water surrounding the body serves to bring us into a deeper space of relaxation. By entering into that deeper space while being surrounded by water creates a sensibility to energy as free flowing and transparent to the body, which has the effect of energising and replenishing the body in natural life energy.

In addition to using the exercises outlined in this book in the normal way, most of them can be practised while being submerged in water to add another dimension to re-balancing your life from the inside out.

The calmness of water transmits itself through us as deep intelligence which we can connect with at the intrinsic level of touch. Since our whole body is a touch body, the surrounding touch of water acts as a natural form of restorative energy presence.

As we notice this and relax into the water's energy, we're also submerging our body, heart and mind into the subtle field of energy that also surrounds and pervades the physical body.

We can allow the body to rest in this deep calm of natural water submersion for extended periods and find, if the space allows it, that our body, mind and heart will feel deeply rested in the natural energy or light that is transmitted through water.

This practice should be engaged on a regular basis to help replenish the body whenever we feel exhausted, collapsed and run down or whenever we need to engage in a non-stimulating yet pleasurable natural energy replenishing experience.

How to Give Energy Rebalancing Treatments to Others

The basic disposition of Conscious Touch is to first be in a state of equanimity and balance through careful study of the general principles outlined in this book and by fully engaging the forms of practices until there is a basic level of proficiency felt energetically and bodily.

The signs of this disposition may include the following:

1. The steadiness of breath in the body with particular focus in the abdominal region below the umbilical scar. Through consistent daily practice of deep breathing, the whole body should begin to feel more rested and calm. The sense of resting in a deep space of calm is synonymous with the state of balance.

2. A state of whole-body relaxation is also signalled as mental, emotional and physical steadiness, therefore attention should be pointed and focused on selfless service with the intention to bring calming energy to the recipient.

3. The feeling of calmness should also be noticed by others, and especially by anyone you intend to serve, by being fully present and simply happy, which is the sign of whole bodily (including emotional and mental) balance.

4. The disposition of serving another consciously is found by surrendering from the heart to the universal-field or prior space of love and happiness.

Therefore, recognise that any healing that takes place, whether it is the release of an emotional, physical or psychological constraint, is not actually caused by the healer directly but is always a sign of the life-force moving more freely through both participants.

That, in turn, may allow for conditions such as mental, emotional or physical tensions, psychological traumas, physical pain and so on to be released.

5. Anyone offering conscious touch to others should feel beyond the sense that they're somehow doing the healing, and instead put benign energy into preparing themselves mentally, emotionally and physically so that their disposition is of simplicity, love, compassion and happiness in the service to others.

It should become obvious when there is a feeling of imbalance and uncertainty, such as feeling physically, mentally or emotionally run down, or through exhibiting signs of physical, emotional or mental toxicity shown as physical weakness or mental and emotional instability, sadness and even psychological depression through the feeling of failure or incompleteness.

If there is any such pattern in one's disposition, it is still possible to offer healing by first bringing the whole body back into a state of balance by engaging the various practices offered and through an intuitive feeling of what the body's needs are.

Bathing in fresh cool or warm water (depending on the climate) and bringing more energy to the lower body through deep breathing can quickly serve to refresh and bring the body up into a regenerative state of equanimity and balance.

The healer is therefore metaphorically something like a transparent reflector or conduit, by allowing the mind and body to be an open vessel that feels and directs the life-force or life-energy with love toward the recipient, then love becomes the premise for the healing and feels beyond even the need to heal.

Conscious Touch and the Laying on of Hands

Preparation

If your body is tense, you can use the system of circular movements to loosen the joints and prepare the body, with an emphasis on the head, neck, shoulders, arms, wrists, hands and fingers. You can also try simply being in, or working with, nature.

Natural environments tend to exist in a more harmonious state of balance than man-made ones, and thus serve to replenish and rebalance the body. In general, any environment you're serving in should be conscious and supportive of positive energy. The environment is as much a part of the feeling dimension as the people in it.

As you prepare to practice the laying on of hands, it's important to allow the patterns of your social/conventional mind to fall away. Enter into a contemplative, meditative space, and remain there for the whole exercise. Allow your natural intuition to guide you before, during and after the session.

This intuition will show you where energy needs to be restored and how to do it. Become like water; an invisible participant, happy and ecstatic. Stay humble by simply surrendering to and enjoying the simplicity of the process.

Now let's look at how to practice the laying on of hands for someone who is physically present. These instructions are primarily written for practice on one person. It is also possible to work with a number of people simultaneously, or with non-humans (animals or subtle beings) and/or within environmental spaces.

If you are involved with serving in this manner, allow your energy to remain open yet focused by embracing the sense of Intrinsic Touch Energy as a universal space while releasing any sense of control of how the process works in, through and as space.

Breathing deeply is essential to maintaining your focus as well as being open to the natural flow of energy balance and rebalance.

Fully embrace the disposition of participant rather than "doer". Recognise that we are not separate from any space we inhabit and if deeply sensitised are felt to be perfectly in tune with subtle energy as space.

- Before you begin, speak to the person you are serving. Find out if they have any physical, mental or emotional symptoms or areas where they feel energy is blocked. If the recipient cannot speak or communicate, simply feel where the energy doesn't seem to be moving.

- Encourage the recipient to come into the session in a zone of contemplation and depth of feeling and to allow their sense of love and happiness to radiate outwardly from the heart. Such a disposition will greatly serve the process of energy-conductivity in their body, as well as your ability to work with them.

- Ask the recipient to lie down, ideally on a massage table. This allows you to move around the body easily. It also allows the person you're working with to be comfortable, which in turn encourages them to drop out and really make themselves available to the process. If you're only doing a short session, the recipient can sit upright in a comfortable, supportive chair.

- Make a gentle feeling-connection to the recipient's body by bringing a soft conscious touch from the forehead and face moving down the frontal line to the bottoms of the feet.

- Place your left hand above the head of the recipient. It's very important to not touch the top of the head during any session. The top part of the head or fontanel point is the gateway to the dimension of spiritual energy that may potentially be received through the blessings of a true spiritual master. For this reason the fontanel point should never be disturbed in this process and modality of energy healing (see glossary for more on the fontanel point).

- Place your right hand on or above the solar plexus or abdominal region.

- Give attention to any areas the recipient has mentioned (or that you have felt) as needing attention.

- Simply feel your connection to the recipient, breathe and allow energy to be felt along the frontal line of the body, and via the spinal line in both yourself and the recipient.

- Your actions and movements should be calm and relaxed.

- Work from the inside out, allowing brightness and happiness to radiate outwards from your heart in all directions.

- Hold this position for a few minutes or longer if you feel like you need to make a deeper connection with the recipient.

- From here, you can work in a number of ways, depending on who you're working with and what you feel they need.

There are three primary ways of working:

- First – by touching the body, pressing lightly but steadily with the hands briefly on each section either in specific or random patterns.

- Second – by laying your hands on a specific location on the body. For this, have the recipient lie on their back. Begin with the face, then move on to the chest, and then the abdominal region. Move right down to the toes. Have the recipient lie on their front, then work back in the opposite direction. Begin with the toes, then work up the legs to the lower back. Follow the spinal line to the back of the head.

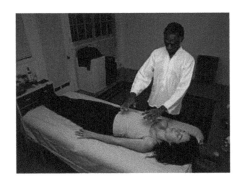

- Third – by moving your hands just above the body, your movements should be calm and slow. Moderate your movements in response to the natural life-energy of your recipient and of your own body along with energy that be felt above and around the of both yourself and the recipient.

- Feel free to combine these techniques in any way that feels right and effective.

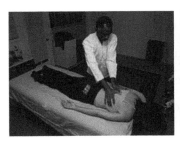 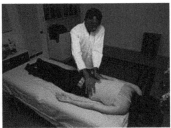

Whatever combination you choose, make sure you are allowing the process and energy to simply flow through you. Let go of any motives to manipulate or force energy in any direction.

A session of the laying on of hands can last anywhere from five minutes to half an hour or longer, depending on the needs of the person or people you're working with, and the feeling you get when working with them.

If you need to ask the person questions for any clarification, do so at the very beginning of the treatment. Ordinarily the session should be silent, which relieves the need to engage the verbal mind and allows the whole body to rest more easefully into receiving the treatment.

You may find there are spontaneous moments when a question will arise to address certain issues during the course of the treatment and you should simply allow for this.

You may feel moved to close your eyes while offering this service. This can occur through feeling drawn into working purely in the space of perceptual feeling as touch. This is a sign of deepening sensitivity during the session.

As you develop your practice of the laying on of hands, you will become increasingly capable of picking up on energetic cues. Some people may find they even develop the subtle capability to actually see energy blockages – often without the recipient being aware that such a blockage actually exists.

The laying on of hands as conscious touch should not be used as a substitute for medical treatment. Likewise, it should not be used as a means to cure illnesses. Use the laying on of hands simply as it is intended: as a means for improving the conductivity of the natural life-force in people and things.

While you should be sensitive to any positive results that arise from your practice of the laying on of hands, you should refrain from seeking any particular result or sign. For this process to be most effective, you need to get out of the way.

No touch can be measured
No design is too large or small
Intrinsic Touch Energy fits all

whether near or far

east or west

north or south

above or below

inside out

outside in

thin

stout

fat

small

tall

big brazen

tiny petite

large

towering

shaking

cowering

devouring

explicitly philandering

courting

cavorting

snorting

farting

dubiously disarming

in ruin with destitution

fly ridden

bed ridden

dense thick

closed off

lost

alone and forgotten

This Touch can find you

can brighten you

to "God knows where"

you are in Touch

as Touch

this much is true

Touch is love

is you

Appendix A

The Body as a Sensory Dynamic

The whole bodily sensory mode of touch is not limited to the depth of our feeling as energetic sensation. When truly observed, we can see that we not only feel as touch but we also breathe and are perceptually aware as touch. The relaxation of the breath allows the body to fall into a depth of the whole body feeling sensibility and awareness as touch.

The body's cellular structure is fundamentally a feeling process, as is the molecular structure of every facet of the whole body, a feeling process. There is no mode of the body as an organism that is not a feeling process. In other words, to be aware we must feel, to notice anything we must relate to it through the dimension that is feeling as touch.

This is always so but for the implications of this understanding to be felt we must go through a deepening in our conscious awareness. We may be consciously aware of the body as a mind or mental perception, or as expressive or suppressive emotion and as physical energy or physical action.

These patterns of a relationship to the body may identify us as a separate object or separate objectified pattern. Being more consciously aware reveals that the body is never limited to these forms of association. We can feel beyond all of these objectified patterns through the process of our conscious awareness as touch.

The body inhabits space but paradoxically the body is itself space, as well as a shape. The space, shape and form of the body exist within and as a sphere of awareness. This can be felt through simply entering into the dimension of feeling as awareness to recognise what the body is as feeling-awareness-sensory-space.

This is potentially an experience of feeling beyond the skin surface to notice the field of energy prior to and beyond yet coincident with the physical body, otherwise known as the etheric field or subtle energy surrounding the entire bodily skin surface as well as flowing within the physical dynamic of the body.

To feel and breathe the body as a sensory space is to also understand that the body exists within the fabric of something far, far greater than its bodily inhabited space. If the body exists in space as space, what is the space within which it inhabits and within which it appears?

That space is feeling consciousness or unlimited, boundless energy that can be felt when the mind is relaxed and the body is allowed to open up as a sensory feeling organic process in its truly natural state.

When we touch we're instantly exercising the body as energy or as an energetic being without use or identification with thought. This is what is meant by sensory awareness, a fundamental and unencumbered natural free state of being.

However, the implication of actually "being touch" suggests that touch is not specifically an activity. Moreover touch is nothing we need to do to be it. It is inherent as the nature of what and who we are without thought, action or even expression. Indeed, the most essential reference is feeling, awareness or being.

What does this mean in our lives? What does this actually mean? How does this understanding implicate who we are and what we do? What difference does it make to us?

In some sense this knowledge may not make any difference to us or paradoxically it may make all the difference in terms of how we see, feel and relate to the world and to each other.

The implications are that "feeling" as the state of awareness in reality is universal and non-separate. In other words, all beings and all things presently alive as energy exist within a dimension of reality that is a universal conscious feeling of energy, not different and owned by anyone or anything.

To live in the manner that this understanding reveals is to completely change the orientation of one's life. A complete turnaround will occur that incorporates the recognition of living within a universal field of conscious energy that is always inter-relational, always flowing to and toward, in and through, and always alive as everything whether visible or invisible.

Touch as a living state when recognised does not create divisions, it is non-divisionism, non-separation, non-difference, Perfect Unity.

This is the catalyst for great and profound change in all human relations beyond religion, culture, identity and conventional knowledge.

Appendix B

The Blessing Touch of Love

The World-Friend Adi Da sensitised me to intrinsic touch many years ago during my first spiritual retreat in December 1990 at Adi Da Samrajashram, Naitauba, Fiji.

Adi Da is no ordinary teacher and I soon found this out after being invited to sit in his company to receive his blessing regard.

In the sitting I was amazed at the purity I felt in Adi Da's physical company. His penetrating gaze was always full of great love and sobriety, a gaze that he freely gave to each of his students.

When his gaze came to me it felt very calming though there was nothing particularly extraordinary about it. I simply felt humanly connected. I received his gaze until his eyes moved to another student.

After that, something mysterious happened where I began to feel drowsy even though prior to the occasion I wasn't feeling tired.

It is well known in the spiritual traditions that a true spiritual master can transmit spiritual energy even via a glance and this was very true in the case of Adi Da.

Following this as I seemed to struggle with receiving his spiritual blessing regard, suddenly I was highly surprised and enriched with a warm sensory feeling around my lower back, like an invisible circular ball of energy that served to rebalance my body as I responded to his transmitted touch by straightening my posture.

There was a feeling of brightness in my heart and love within the touch that immediately relieved the drowsiness I was feeling. I turned to see if anyone had touched my back, but it was obvious that no one had moved at all.

After the occasion a senior member of Adi Da's inner circle came to me with a message from Adi Da. He said, "You should always keep your legs crossed at the ankles when sitting in a chair."

I smiled in response and realised that Adi Da was also reminding me how to best conduct his transmission of blessing by maintaining my form in a stable asana or posture.

Every student sitting in Adi Da's blessed company has a unique story to tell of his spiritual blessing service with them. I was fortunate to be one among many to feel the magnitude and power of Adi Da's immense giving of love to everyone that truly transformed and brightened my life.

Appendix C

The Essence of Touch

Touch is in some sense a most profound mystery. All of the words in this book are given as a means to explore the vast depth that is touch.

Is there an essence or source of touch that when located changes the way we consider what it is?

In my own discovery, the essence and obvious source of touch was revealed to me through the relationship to my teacher and spiritual master Adi Da Samraj (1939-2008).

Adi Da has literally shown me that the body is not merely identifiable as some kind of impenetrable solid object, but rather, beyond this common conception of being the body is the understanding that feels and recognises the body as conscious awareness and therefore the body as an energy process that is never really fixed as any kind of solid anything.

By his graceful spiritual presence, which I feel as a profound depth of touch, Adi Da has opened a gateway into his domain of free feeling and directed my heart and entire being there, where reality can be felt as expanded sensory awareness wherein the deeper sensory space of touch is known as a tacit, non-verbal, instinctive and intuitive-feeling process.

Every day of my life is therefore informed in some manner by Adi Da's spiritual touch through entering into communion with his divine, bright spiritual presence and state.

The word "bright" is who Adi Da is, in his indivisible form. Adi Da is known as the "Bright", which is a literal description of his state of person beyond the appearance of His human body which passed away in November 2008.

In essence it is a divine gift of blessing felt at the heart that Adi Da has revealed to me, most tangibly through the grace of his divine spiritual touch.

When I sit and commune with Adi Da during formal occasions of meditation and in any spontaneous moment of conscious awareness, my whole being feels completely overwhelmed by this deeper space of touch; energetically, subtly, spiritually and without any words or actions.

The body and its entire space and beyond are literally captured into the depth of vulnerability which is the catalyst for the development and offering of Intrinsic Touch Energy as an energy rebalancing practice.

This sense of touch as space without words, flows as subtle conscious energy, informing every aspect of the physical, mental and emotional state of the body via and prior to the breath.

The ordinary sensibility of physical touch enters into a space that can be called reality consciousness or living light. Touch itself is felt more profoundly as consciousness; the space that exists as the living light or radiant all-pervading energy.

It is a dropping out of ordinary body awareness and a deepening embrace of the divinely radiant conscious feeling that is in essence and ultimately the bright radiance of Adi Da!

Appendix D

Bonus green drink recipes

Re-balance Your Life from the Inside Out with Blended Green Smoothies.

Diet is an important part of how energy moves through the body based on the type and quality of food we consume and how that food is assimilated.

Our general state of equanimity and balance may to a large extent be dependent on our dietary choices.

I have found over the years that green smoothies made preferably with organic produce, serves to cleanse and open up the body. Green smoothies can act to fully replenish the body from the inside out and to a certain extent enhance sensory awareness and touch as a sensitivity guide that serves to rest the body in its natural happy state.

The suggested recipes below can be used to experiment with your normal diet. Feel free to try out other green smoothie recipes if these do not work for you.

3 Recipes
BANANA, APPLE, GINGER

2 ripe bananas, a bunch of kale leaves, 1 apple, 1 small handful cilantro, 1 small piece fresh ginger (crushed), 2 cups purified water

MANGO WEEDS

2 mangos; 1 handful edible weeds such as lambs quarters, stinging nettles, or purslane; 2 cups purified water

STRAWBERRY, BANANA, ROMAINE

1 cup strawberries, 2 bananas, ½ bunch romaine, 2 cups purified water

- Always use organic produce where possible
- Use a high-powered blender such as:
  Vitamix
  JTC OmniBlend 1

Suggested readings for Diet and Health:

Green Gorilla by Adi Da Samraj
Raw Food Made Easy (for 2 people) by Jennifer Cornbleet
The Green Smoothie by Victoria Boutenko
Green Smoothie Retreat by Victoria Boutenko

Glossary

Adi – Sanskrit for "first", "primordial", "source" – also "primary", "beginning". Thus, most simply, "Adi Da" means "First Giver".

Adi Da – the "First Giver" or "Divine Giver".

(Adi Da) Samraj – in Sanskrit "Sam – harmonious" "Raj - King or emperor or sovereign ruler".

Adi Da Samrajashram – The Island of Naitauba is the primary Spiritual Retreat Sanctuary established by Adi Da Samraj in Fiji.

Adidam – a spiritual practice revealed by Adi Da Samraj.

Ashram – a set-apart place for spiritual practice.

Chi (Qi, Mana, Prana, universal life-force) – invisible pervading force flowing through things.

Communion – a form of relationship felt as love in its most profound essence in connection with the divine.

Consciousness – unlimited awareness of feeling.

Constraints – forms of tensions or energy blocks that obstruct energy flow.

Cyclically – cycles of the natural breath.

Da – is a traditional name for father in Sanskrit. It simply means "giver" or "to give". Da is also used as a referent for the Divine. In essence, the **Divine** is the "primary giver or primary source" of happiness, truth and light.

Elemental – a holistic form made up of its elemental parts, for example: wind, fire, water, air, the human body.

Energy blocks – (see Constraints).

Energy Field – energy that is subtle and felt to pervade or surround the physical body.

Epiphany – a moment of sudden revelation or great realisation.

Etheric (Etheric field/energy) – the chi body or subtle energy body, that surrounds, pervades and is coincident with the physical body.

Fiji – a country in the South Pacific, which is an archipelago of more than 300 islands. It is famed for rugged landscapes, palm-lined beaches and coral reefs with clear lagoons.

Fontanel – also spelt fontanelle, the soft spot in the skull of an infant, covered with a tough, fibrous membrane. There are six such spots at the junctions of the cranial bones. The lateral fontanels close within three months of birth, the posterior fontanel at about two months, and the anterior fontanel by two years.

The anterior fontanel is also said to be the point of spiritual descent and ascent of the spiritual anatomy of the body. The spirit body descends via this point during the process of birth and ascends via this point during the process of death.

God – the supreme or ultimate reality, indivisible and indefinable.

Horticulture/ Horticulturalist – the science and art of growing fruits, vegetables, flowers, or ornamental plants.

Knots – a tight constriction or the sense of constriction.

Intrinsic – the essential nature (in the context of this book) a means of access to the very source of touch.

Light – radiant energy or brightness felt via the heart, the literal feeling of open-hearted happiness felt throughout the whole body and beyond. Esoterically it is understood that everything is light.

Life-energy (Life-force) – the force that pervades all life.

Perception – the holistic use of the senses to open more deeply into the dimension of feeling.

Presence – the quality of emanation within, through and as the dimension of feeling.

Qigong – Qi (or chi) is energy, gong means practice or discipline. Qigong is the discipline and practice of conducting qi (life-energy) for health and well-being.

Radiate (Radiating from the heart) – radiating from the heart is a conscious choice to feel and express love as feeling in all relations.

Reality – the state of things as they actually exist, as opposed to an idealistic or notional idea of them. Exploring Intrinsic Touch is another means to enter into a deeper understanding of reality.

Sensory – bringing deeper awareness through the feeling senses of the whole body including the five senses.

Shiatsu – "she – finger" and "atsu – pressure" is the practice of finger pressure on the acupuncture points of the body to create balance and harmony.

Spiritual – to be of spirit, an intangible state prior to and sometimes coincident with the physical body.

Spiritual touch – the capability to communicate, transmit or receive spiritual energy as subtle touch.

Spiritual presence – feeling a presence that is prior to bodily awareness associated with great spiritual teachers and spiritual masters.

Transmission – everyone transmits some form of energy. However, transmission in this context refers to adepts or spiritual masters who transmit a more profound level of energy for the purpose of awakening others to realise their state.

Treatment Testimonials

Mary Wells

Horticulturalist, gardener

Taveuni Island, Fiji

I received a treatment from Colin in Intrinsic Touch Energy, I found it to be extremely beneficial and incredibly relaxing.

During the second half of the treatment, I relaxed so deeply that I dropped into a deep meditative state of mindlessness.

Everything totally quieted down, there was no thinking and all the edges of my body felt erased. There was no demarcation between my body and the rest of the universe.

It isn't often that I feel that and it was really helpful in putting me in touch whole bodily with the greater Reality of our existence, that we are not separate, self-contracted individuals but exist in a state of unity and seamless wholeness with all of life. And I felt great afterwards!

It is a very integrative and rejuvenating experience for both your body and your soul.

Renata Hercog

Personal Development and Business Consultant

London, UK

When Colin introduced me to an Intrinsic Touch Energy session, for the first time in my life I didn't know what to expect, but I discovered the real new world within me.

After only one month of following his instructions and doing the practice daily for 15 minutes, my clarity of thought and concentration improved significantly.

My life has become much calmer, I feel more relaxed and able to manage the daily stress of a very busy work and social life.

Rachel Key
Registered nurse
Auckland, NZ

Colin gave me an Intrinsic Touch Energy treatment recently. I would highly recommend his work. The treatment was very powerful yet gentle. To me, that is a winning combination.

The subtle energy rebalancing treatment worked on several levels at once for me. Physically I had a healing moment in a particular muscle, this completely surprised me as the touch is gentle and not a massage.

But then a bit later, there was an emotional and psychological release of a grief issue that had periodically surfaced, however, prior to receiving this treatment, I hadn't been aware that this emotion was held in a particular area of my body.

With Colin's focus and calm, the emotion of it just quietly released. I felt fully safe in his hands. I feel quite clear that anyone would feel safe in his hands because it is tacitly obvious he connects to a very calm state whilst he is working with you.

I fully recommend his sense and healing touch to every/any one.

Susie Bagshawe
Shiatsu practitioner
Taveuni Island, Fiji

The Intrinsic Touch Energy treatment was very powerful, it allows the body to release energetic contractions of muscle and nerve which in-turn allows for a deep sense of internal relaxation.

I was overall restored and renewed in my sense of energy focus and balance.

Acknowledgements

I would like to acknowledge my dear friend and colleague Frederick Court. Frederick is a talented speaker, trained acupuncturist, professional actor, writer and artistic visionary.

His suggestions and considerations regarding the thread and direction of this book have been invaluable. He suggested many additions and changes through the creative process of our dialogue and gave invaluable editing.

The book cover was sourced and edited by Julien Lesage, an extraordinary designer and talented poet.

The images were taken by two photographers; the bare feet images by Lyn Houghton, and the outdoor grass by Andrew Riddoch. Thank you, guys, for the time and energy you gave in producing these beautiful images.

Many thanks to Susie Bagshawe, Marisse Lee, Alexandra Makris, David Andreae, Frank Marerro and Rachel Key for all your feedback, reviews and commentaries that have helped the development of this work.

About the Author

Colin Boyd was born on January 22nd 1962 in South London, United Kingdom. He is a devotee for over 30 years of the world-renowned spiritual master and world teacher Adi Da Samraj (1939–2008).

As part of his spiritual practice of the Reality-Way of Adidam revealed and taught by Adi Da, Colin has studied devotional yoga, hatha yoga, Qigong and sacred theatre. Throughout the early years of his time in Adi Da's company, Colin received direct guidance and instruction from Adi Da in matters of spiritual conductivity, sacred dance, mime theatre, as well as many other areas of human growth and spiritual practice.

Colin has been a keen student of various forms of dance and mime theatre for over 25 years. He began his education in dance in the United Kingdom in 1984 with a dance group called the Original Phoenix, who went on to win a televised dance competition that year. In 1987 Colin worked with a UK-based mime company Black Mime Theatre, before going on to create and perform his own mime shows. He went on to teach his own style of dance/mime theatre workshops to children and adults throughout the UK, Fiji and the US.

Colin is currently based in Fiji and lives on a spiritual retreat at Adi Da Samrajashram, Naitauba Island, Fiji, Adi's Da's principal sacred hermitage ashram. He previously lived and studied there from 1997 to 2006, where he first began to develop a sensitivity to the subtle energy process associated with Adi Da's spiritual blessing.

He continued his studies in spiritual practice at Adi Da's spiritual residence in Northern California, the Mountain of Attention Sanctuary from 2006–2011. After this period of intensive focus in Adi Da's sacred forms which also included immersing himself in sacred theatre, primarily focused in the production and performance of Adi Da's contemporary liturgical drama *The Mummery* with the First Room Theatre Guild, a deeper manifestation of Intrinsic Touch Energy was revealed.

With new insight, he returned to the UK for three and a half years where he further considered, developed and taught the process of Intrinsic Touch Energy to friends and students in the UK.

In more recent years, he has continued to develop the process and platform for the practice of Intrinsic Touch Energy through the form of this book *You Are Touch*, which is a summary understanding and guidance for the practice of Intrinsic Touch Energy, a process that is directly informed by the spiritual blessing received through the grace of his relationship to Adi Da Samraj.

About Adi Da Samraj (1939 - 2008)

Unique spiritual realiser, teacher, author, artist, and world-friend.

Adi Da Samraj devoted His life to the realisation and communication of Truth – what He called the 'Bright', Prior Unity or the Indivisible Reality in which we all appear.

He communicated that Truth through many means – literary, artistic and spiritual. His numerous books of spiritual, philosophical, social and practical wisdom are widely acknowledged as among the most insightful spiritual teachings of the modern world. His artistic works – including many monumental-scale images – are exhibited in key locations around the world.

During His lifetime, Adi Da touched and transformed the lives of many thousands of secular and religious seekers, founding a new sacred tradition – the Reality-Way of Adidam – for those who respond most seriously to His spiritual calling, and enter into a formal devotional and spiritual relationship with Him.

He empowered a number of sanctuaries around the world to function as places of pilgrimage and retreat in perpetuity. In response to his wisdom and blessings, sacred centres and foundations have been established internationally. Through all these gifts and more, Adi Da's blessing communication continues to be powerfully active and alive.

https://www.adidasamraj.org/

Useful websites and links:

www.daplastique.org

www.da-peace.org

www.adidaupclose.org

www.adidafoundation.org

www.conductivityhealing.com

www.dawnhorsepress.com

Suggested readings of Adi Da Samraj:

The Knee Of Listening

The Reality Way of Adidam

My Bright Word

Not-Two Is Peace

The Aletheon

Conductivity Healing

Green Gorilla: The Searchless Raw Diet

Reviews for You Are Touch

Colin's book *You Are Touch* presents his deepest understanding of touch from a unique point of view, a point of view that comes from many years of living as a devotee of his "Heart Master Adi Da Samraj" and from his immersion in the culture that is a part of his life as a devotee.

He presents some of the oldest forms of Traditional Qigong Practices in a new light, one based on a more feeling awareness of the essence of these practices so that rather than just being a sterile physical exercise they become a process of allowing the body to deeply feel in touch with what he calls "The Radiant Field of All-Pervading Energy". Of course the various postures and movements are not the point of his book, but as Colin goes on to describe they are a guide to allowing the body to open to Intrinsic Touch Energy as a deepening practice of feeling into and beyond our conventional limits.

Colin has also developed his own unique style of practice that he feels has given him a way to connect with and even communicate this feeling of Universal Touch to others in a healing environment based on His Master Instructions.

Paul Litchfield and Jane Yang
Chi gong Therapy Centre, Australia

Let me suggest that Colin's "You Are Touch" is an invitation to touch and be touched by the cosmic unity, in prior harmony with the all-pervading energy, the love that fills and is our every breath.

I love the practicality and physicality mixed with the sublime with the spiritual with the poetry of rap, lyricism, Upanishad and nursery rhyme.

I read Colin's book lying on my back on the sofa in the early morning light. I wasn't meaning to physically exercise just read, but the poetry and rhythm and transmission of enthusiasm, harmony and joy through the words and pictures and texture had me rolling my arms and ankles and slithering my hands and fingers like water snakes and breathing like I imagine a dolphin might breathe, not just through the blowholes of a mouth and nose but through the skin, through the heart, through the doors and windows and the walls.

Simon Pritchard
www.saatchiart.com

What do you look for when you read a book without consideration of its genre?

I personally look for the following qualities:

It must be easy to read and understand.

It must be entertaining.

It must have certain credibility and integrity, either by virtue of the author's personal knowledge and/or by virtue of extensive research.

The book, *You Are Touch*, has all those characteristics. It actually reminded me of how children's books are...easy and fun to read. What makes it charming is the fact that the author incorporated poetry in an otherwise technical type of book. So, if you are looking for a healthy physical regime with rhymes of poetry on the side, then this is perfect for you.

Moreover, practically applying the touch exercises here gave me a better understanding of the depth and universality of the word "touch". I was fascinated by the part that discussed listening to the heartbeat and breathing. What can I say? You have to try it to comprehend my meaning. And if you are a seeker of sorts, then you get to obtain a free lecture about reality and being as well…in simple words.

Marissa Lee
Writer
Harping_by_a_Pixie - blog

As an actor I've learnt over the years how to prepare myself before going on stage to give a performance. There is something about preparing the body to reach beyond ourselves to find the depth and integrity of who or whatever we're playing to touch the audience in some way.

Colin's book tackles this relationship in a direct and profound way, with practical exercises that allow for a deeper sense of mystery and being to come forth. As actors we have to feel a profound connection with the mystery that is behind the act, which is the True Heart of the Self in order to relate to ourselves and to others in a way that brings real meaning to the everyday actions of our lives.

Colin's book brings real instruction on how to connect with this 'waking essence' from the body through to the mind and into the 'Heart of being Itself'. Life is about relationship, limber up with this book and the touch of the profound to the deepest of levels.

Jym Daly
Artistic Director of Fidget Feet
International touring and award winning Theatre Company